Haunting

Poems

Larissa Matharu

To Connie
With love and gratitude
Larissa Matharu
x

Haunting Poems

Larissa Matharu

Paperback Edition First Published in the United Kingdom
in 2017 by aSys Publishing

eBook Edition First Published in the United Kingdom
in 2017 by aSys Publishing

ISBN: 978-1-910757-95-6

aSys Publishing
http://www.asys-publishing.co.uk

Illustrations by Phil Lockwood

Other Paintings by kind permission of Liz Balkwill PS AFAS IEA,
Phil Lockwood and a gift from Prof John Bastin MA PhD FRAS;
also a gift from the late Audrey Schwartz

Front Cover Painting Enigma by Phil Lockwood

Back Cover Painting Larissa and Theology by
Prof John Bastin MA PhD FRAS

Artists Model: Larissa Matharu BA Hons QCG mCDI

http://www.hauntingpoems.co.uk
BlandingsandMarple@hushmail.com

Contents

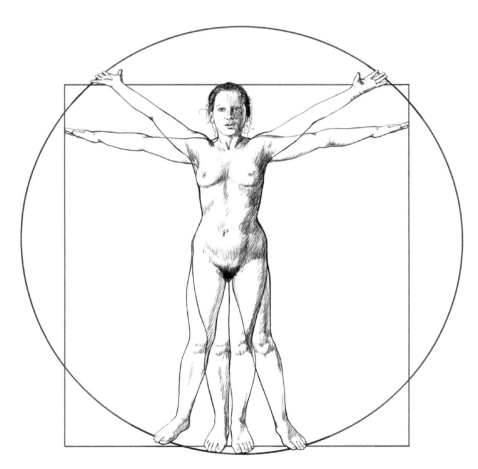

Leonardo Tribute by Phil Lockwood.

Dedication

To the paediatricians, psychiatrists, general practitioners and counsellors who saved my life and who afforded me physical and emotional sanctuary: Dr Deepak Kalra, Dr L Chang, Dr Marian Foley, Dr Solomon, Dr W Ahmed and all your colleagues, I will never forget your salvation, wisdom, compassionate dedication and TLC. *Gratias vobis ago.*

For my teachers at Neachells Lane Infant School, Wednesfield High School, Loreto College Manchester, Richard Huish College Taunton, University of Greenwich and Manchester Metropolitan University. I am indeed fortunate and utterly grateful to have met the most thought-provoking, wonderful, fantastic and devoted teachers. In thought and deed, you are cherished daily.

To James who sacrificed everything to rescue and protect me and to reveal to me the depth of Christ's spiritual healing. You are the brightest shining star and I am forever in your debt.

For the artists I have modelled for – Phil Lockwood, Prof John Bastin MA PhD FRAS, Liz Balkwill PS AFAS IEA, Peter Wardle, Preeti Shenoy – and all the other artists I have had the honour to pose for. I feel that through life, costume and portraiture modelling, through your art, we are putting right all the harm that was done against my body and being. Your art is indeed treasure. Thank you for making my body and mind better. I find life modelling incredibly therapeutic and immensely liberating.

To the astrologers Tony Hyland and Robert Currey and the chirologist Johnny Fincham - your wisdom and enlightenment has been life-changing, life-enhancing and life-saving.

For Arthur and Mary Little.

For PDB: 'Plato is my friend, Aristotle is my friend but my greatest friend is truth.' Sir Isaac Newton.

For my late friends, Audrey Schwartz, Anthony Francis Jordan (descendant of the Bishop of Exeter and Theologian Richard Hooker), Mary and Wallace Beeston, Michael Jamieson Bristow, John Hudd, Michael John Kench and Mr I F Kilmister, your deaths have been devastating and the world is a more lonely place without your souls but I know that you are in Heaven looking on lovingly. Thank you for your Heavenly love and support.

To the Holy Trinity, thank you for answering my prayers!

Introduction

I read Theology at The University of Greenwich and studied for the Postgraduate Diploma in Careers Guidance and Qualification in Careers Guidance at Manchester Metropolitan University; it was my dream to go to university and this dream kept me going throughout my traumatic childhood.

As well as being an artists' model and poet, I am a careers adviser. I have worked as a special educational needs and disabilities careers adviser (SEND), working in special and mainstream schools and colleges, supporting young people and their families. I am honoured to have been able to work in this profession alongside such devoted and dedicated teachers and colleagues to help our clients and students – whom I think of often.

I have also enjoyed volunteering with a number of organisations.

I suffer from PTSD and I use a range of methods to cope and manage my symptoms and flashbacks.

I am donating 100 % of the royalties from every purchase of this poetry book to the charity NAPAC – National Association for People Abused in Childhood. I want to give something back for all the help I have received and in doing so, help others. I am grateful to NAPAC for accepting my offer.

The views and opinions expressed in this poetry book are my own and not those of NAPAC or any other organisation or persons.

Thank you for purchasing *Haunting Poems* and I hope my poetry book takes you on an interesting journey!

Larissa Matharu BA Hons QCG mCDI

Portrait by Liz Balkwill PS AFAS IEA.

Haunted Saturdays

What do you know when you are four and five years old
What do you know about sexual abuse
Nothing
There is nothing to understand

There are no words
No adjectives no nouns no verbs
Just actions and doings
Their actions their doings
Doings to me

My body
And their body
Her body Her face
Her ugly contorted orgasmic face
And my body
Her actions Her doings
against my body
against my eyes
against my hands
my little five year old hands

What is there to see
Haunts ceaselessly
and lives relentlessly
for all eternity

Tears and flashbacks
Immersed in every day and
All of daily living
That which will never cease
Until Death Us Do Part

My friend The Grim Reaper
Who Will One Day
Pour his healing balm of death
Upon these tears
Upon these haunting pictures
cemented and imprisoned in my mind - holding it all together

And on that day
They will become free
Free ghosts in the secret mists of time and
This dark and sinister secret game she played
will be no more locked in my mind

Like the sunshine
Like the blue sky
Like the Chocolate Buttons
The rustle of green leaves and luscious grass and
Nature thriving all around

What do you know when you are four and five years old
What do you know about sexual abuse
Nothing
There is nothing to understand

Consent

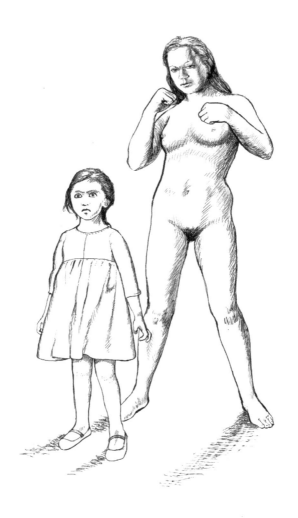

Consent
Who gave you my consent?
Oh, I see the Devil gave
It wasn't me
you my consent
It wasn't me . . .

Satisfied?
Hungry for more?
Well, GO ON THEN
TAKE ME
USE ME
TAKE MORE OF MY BODY
USE MY BODY
TAKE IT
USE IT
GO ON . . .

Oh, I get it, You don't want my body now
It's not the same
It's not little
It's not infantile
It answers back
This body answers back
It's not the same
It's got hair!!! ry
It's got ship - shape

Scared?
You should be
Where was my consent?
Oh yes, I forget, the Devil gave you my consent

Well my friend, abuser
My mate the Grim Reaper
is plucking consent
from your hands and that of your friend Satan's.

Scared?
You should be
Five year olds Do Not Consent
Consent to sex with an adult
an adult female
Get It?

But that's just it
The beauty and pleasure of it for you
Isn't It?
Five year old girls, pure, innocent, little, infantile, non - consenting

Consent
What A Word . . . It doesn't even exist for a five year old
Get It?

Fulgere Memoria Sanctum

Oh joy of joys
Chocolate Buttons - Yummy
Their little shiny purple bag slithering with Humpty Dumpty or
Hickory Dickory dock . . . Wow! All for me . . . Really?

Then I gaze up to your face as you place them in my hands
I open them full of disbelief
I don't know why
Should I eat them
Can I eat them
Are they really for me?
But it's Chocolate I Love
So you pop them in my mouth
sealing them with wicked lips
evil stealing in my mouth
My Chocolate . . . HELP . . . IT'S MY CHOCOLATE . . . stolen

Camera Camera
Like a camera shot - all distorted
segmented pictures in my mind
Flashbacks - Why?
Why not whole picture memories?
Why Why Why like distorted segmented camera shots filmed and
printed in my mind - Why not whole?

I don't see
I can't see - Why?
But I see
your face
But Why Can't I see
All your strange big woman body
you're too big and I'm too little
your hands and my little 5 year old hands

All I see
I see is eye level
your vagina
your hands
my hands
my vagina
your breasts take me to audio, I hear it doesn't care
your voice ordering me
When I fail, it gets angry
I'm not strong enough
I can't do it
Where's my bodily strength?
I'm only little - can't you see
I'm tired

My mind's camera shots - it's my eye level
Pictures segmemted
distorted
not all of you . . . get it?
you're too big, I'm too little

It's my mind's camera eye
all it
photographs
your vagina
your hands
your pubic hair
my hands
my vagina
your breasts
your voice telling me off . . . God and Police coming to get
me . . . trouble dooms looms loud like clapping thunder
Scared . . . me I'm

Your Power
My Life
your hands

like knives
your hands your fingers
like knives stuck inside

Where Are You My Surgeon?
When will you come?
Are You Skilled Enough?
Are You Clever Enough?
It's okay
Fly Away Surgeon
These knives you see
her hands her fingers stuck inside my soul
these knives
beguile my smile, my beaming smile
my big shiny eyes
my idiotic brain
that can't count
doesn't know left from right
can't hold maps - clueless on maps

Has a map
of her body
and my little 6 year old body

Camera eye shots
distorted
segmented
my eye level you see
it's my eye level
These pictures fragmented shards of stabbing
glass in my brain it doesn't work - it hurts

But my Lovers
I See All of You
I See All Your Body
How Glorious
and all of my body
it's my eye level
you see
it's grown
it's my eye level - it's taller
Your NOT segmented broken fragmented distorted images
Your Body Is Whole
Your Big Strong Chest
Those Beautiful Muscular Arms I Love to Kiss - I cling onto
Those strange flat nipples my lips envelop
My body you hold
Your Body I caress

My Word - Good God
Why the Discordance?

My 7 year old
my 8 year old memories
broken
distorted
fragmented pictures
of her strange knifing body
cutting my body

Behold my Lovers Kiss
Dreamy Big Eyes
Strong Chest
Beautiful Sanctum Arms
Gorgeous Hair
Kind Loving Hands
Your Sweet Tender Thighs - I snuggle into
and Tall Strong Yummy Phallus
Oh Yes Please!

But it's okay my Surgeon
Who ever you are?
Where ever you are?
You may go you're not wanted you're not welcome
The Door is Locked
Have you the Key?
Do you want the Key?
Are you skilled enough?
Are you clever enough?
Happy enough?

These knives her hands
my Hands betrayed
My Body
My Mind
Betrayed
Hello Grim, my friend, Where art thou sweet slumbering sting
today . . . !
My mate . . . Shall we go for a walk?
Lets meander through this blood stained field
Stomp our way across
All smiling
laughing
crying
singing
Pretending there's no distorted fragmented pictures
As if?

It's only
Time and Memories
So What?

But That What . . .
Is Heart and Power
Now What?

1 Peter 1:16 - A Command and A Promise . . . !

Sanctifying my hands,
Sanctifying my eyes,
My ears and my nose
My mouth, legs and feet,
Sanctifying breasts, chest, stomach,
Sanctifying my hair,
My bottom,
Sanctifying my Vagina,
The Blood of Jesus,
Washes these wounds . . .
Ridding my body of
Satan's corrupting claw . . .
The Blood of Jesus.
The most precious gift in the universe . . .

Memory Shots

What was she doing?
What was she Doing? I have to ask
What was she doing having sex with a four year old? What was she
Doing?
I ask Angular, Peculiar Why?

Grotesque Smells Shots
Captured Decades Later
Enlighten in Sex Smells Shock
But My Lovers smell sweetly divine - A Saintly Scent
Hmm

Pubic Hair Protruding Pubic Hair Intruding
Invading
Killing Childhood Hands
Murdering Childhood Eyes
Big Blossoming Eyes - Murdered
Seek n' Search Resurrection - Ongoing
Big Blossoming Eyes Smile Locked n' Loaded Accosting Tainted Shots

Hands Lead, Leading the Way
Upon Body Landscapes Unknown
Peculiar Angular
Memory Shots, Memory Shots
Thou Art Fractured
In Bodies
Wet Smells
Mouths Flood
Grunting Speed Orderly
In Shushing shh Secret Sinisters
God and Police Punishments Await

Pubic Hair, Pubic Hair, Golden Straw Coloured
Pubic Hair Strange
Please Leave Me Alone
Wet and Squidgy, Sticky
Peculiar, Angular
Sinister Secrets of Golden Straw Fur
Hair Pubic Scary
Please Leave Me Alone

12th October 1987

The abusers hand struck across my face;
my mothers hand bled,
her mouth screaming out
"I wish you were dead."
Swallowing a cocktail of drugs
I lay in hospital dying.
"Happy Birthday!" smiled the doctor
"I don't want to go home, please don't send me." I whispered
"That's alright."
"Really?"

12th October 1992

The pain of a birthday seeping through
Short, sharp, striking pain
Into the stomach
Enter the mind
Burning out of my delicate heart.

Behold the pain must seep
The pain must burn
The pain must bury

Years ripple
Decades arrive
Thus saith the Lord: A decade of victory
of hope
of love of life!
Happy Birthday!

A Dedication

My Doctors taught me to live
and not to be suicidal
They taught me to talk when I feel suicidal

My Teachers taught me to smile
Taught me to be happy,
Taught me to live - showed me How to live
Gave me love
Gave me confidence
My Teachers helped me to discover myself.

My friends taught me to love
To love myself as I love them
My friends showed me happiness
And gave me memories
OH, But, HAPPY memories . . .

The family taught me hurt
and the feeling of pain
The family taught me guilt
and worthlessness

But that's all over now
For I have learnt . . .

To be assertive
To talk when I feel suicidal
To smile
To be happy
To live
To have confidence
To love
And feel love
To discover myself...
Eureka.

Gratias vobis ago !

New Years Eve 1992

Droplets of pain
Pain of droplets . . .
Falling, falling, falling,

Jesus,
please catch . . . these
droplets of pain
and wash this
Sea of mine clean . . .

As Big As The Bad Has Been, As Big The Good Will Be

When I was little
Ponderous Questions
Did Summon My Mind

In gravelled concrete paths
strewn across bluebells under
mysteriously cruel arched rainbows
landscaping terraces and framing factory funnels

Enshrined in bleak blackness
my little groping mind gazed upon the future unknown

How delicately dangerous
How missions sweetly impossible
These paradigm dreams that scraped
the shifting sky

... of Art Freedom and Nudity
of University Lecturing Libraries
of blonde blue eyed Englishmen

But of Class, Religion, Spirits and Culture
All lies, lies, lies, lies
Did Battle with
Pinching shards of British steel
hammering my mind as nails of truth
I could not deny ...

The warm enticement of dark church and pub
Cricket and Flirty robes
Soul Scary
Spirit Evoking and as Incantating

Ear Spanking
Life Revolutionary
Magic Music and Effervescent Books
Relaying in song and word

A scythe of death . . .
to concete gravel
to the blasted bondage of forced marriage . . .
it's ghastly gold and sari streams flowing with swords
of Bollywood hypocrisy and
Cognitive Torture embedding sinister flashbacks

HALT . . . !

ALAS . . .

Life is very strange . . .
Thus it's wonder and awe
This Wheel of Karma and Destiny
Which Pulls and Pushes Us
Like Newton's Laws of Motion
To What End . . . ?
To Where . . . ?
The Mystery and Surprise of it all
The gods cheekily hide . . .

Jam

What is this life?
Where are we going?

Hmm this question it scorches - searing
Through our subconscious
We grapple

How splendiferous
This vast empty openess
Crammed, bursting - brimming with folks, with people
On this soiled Earthy promenade.

Interjected with flights of demon evil and angel good
Angel - Demon wings flight and fight betwixt
Our Father Whom Art In Heaven Hallowed Be Thy Name Thy Kingdom
Come Thy Will Be Done On Earth As It Is In Heaven . . .

Pricks Our Kisses and Waves, Betrothed with Smiles
And Hands that Lie unto Hands that betray
Hands that signal Betrayal in Fingertip Nuances Waving Goodbye

Vast Empty Openess
Crammed, bursting with Traffic Jams
Jams of People, Jams Awake, Jams Alert,
Jams Asleep and Fooled lying with sun kissed treachery and
Jams of Graceful Bellowing and Merciful Mellowing Arms
Strawberry, Rasberry - Rose Champagne, Apricot, Marmalade
Lime - Seville, English Cathedral Aspired . . .

What Flavour Art Thou Kisses?
What Flavour Art Thou Arms?
Those Waves of Goodbye?
Thy Scent?
Who In This Life?

What is this Life?
Where Are We Going?
What Flavour Jam Art Thou?
Where Are You Going?
Intermingling with music mayhem and planetary interjectures
Conjuring fates and kismet pleasures with the
Corupting dance of sin and flesh
Erupting with enlightenment

Who in this Life?

Spreads You
Licks You
Covets You?
Leaves You Mould ridden and Fungus rich?

Who - What Picks You?
Why - How?

What Jam Are You?
Which Jam Dost Thou Desire?
Jams all Crammed together
choking, suffocating, space - marginalised
For Lips and Hands to Touch and Smoulder Into . . .

Crumpet,
Muffin,
Toast,
Buttered,
Scone or Scorned?
Praying?

Heaving, Scorching, Searing Dusk Scorched questions
Spinning Headlong
Endless questions Potted and Labelled Thus Lidded
Banning This Ponderous Wonder
Hence Life Influxes with Demons Angels and Choral Evensong . . .

Sanctity

Sanctity
Where is the Sanctity of Life?
Tis a Human Being
The Human Being before you

Their Arms and Hands reaching out
Pulling in, Pulling Back, Reaching Out
Whose Eyes and Lips meander through
This maze, this evergreen maze
Punctuated with Ugly dollars and
The mocking ghost of time

Reaching in, Pulling Out, Pulling in
Time punctuating the Sanctity of Life
Here a minute, gone a second
Now you touch, now you lose

Its impossibility
Time shattering
Fabricating the
Felicitations of the Sanctity of Life
Shades and Shards of memories
Polarising eyes and grabbing limbs

Sanctity . . .

Love, Andrew and 1 John 3 v18

In This Lord's Green and Pleasant Land
There Lies Hidden
A dark despairing
quenched - drowning soul
in Suffocating Earth.

Therein orgasmic stirrings and
organic numb - skulling movements disperse
Gently trickling whilst
Astral sprinkling hovers flying over nipping buds
in this Lord's green and pleasant land

Railway mission troops
swing and rally forth amidst
Ethereal Rocking
Penetrating Blood
Oozing the quenched drowning despairing soul
in this suffocating lord's green and pleasant land

Within unburdening these secret walls
Lies the seemingly impossible . . .
Slaying the anger - anguish
Slashing the bleeding frustration
Sewing the needling pain and
Shooting the whirl of despair

Tender pressurising hands do
irksome ripping shredding and pulling
in the core of a far away soul
in this dark damp suffocating earth

Delicate sharp unshed tears
As streams of knives
Inch their cutting way
Into this bleeding delicate burning heart
Slicing the vials of anger - anguish
Delving through fields of furious frustration

External Earth Invasions
Permeate forlorness
A smile
A handshake
A trickle of laughter
The Clockwork Get Togethers
March solidlly like Roman Numerals
and Centurions tick, tock, tick tock
Whilst despair lingers caught in a web imprisoned

The Abyss opens . . .
and the discontented disconnected drowning soul whirls
in wasteland fears and devastated years
firing arrows and drumming strumming lightning spears
skylines feel and gears whisk
Behold the pain scorched n' burining
Behold the flowering passion
Their ghostly tingling slippery cloak, shimmering, sparkling
flowing from the solar - lunar scape in
Mingling tingling with silken skinscapes
and interlocking spirits.

Profound

It listens
It feels
Touches and Reaches
Out, out, out
Trickling down tears
Bellowing laughter
Bursting balloons
Perceiving, pinching, growing
Enthusiasm gushing
Flowing charm
Silencing the anger
Enriching the Peace

As musical notes dancing on purple air ...

The Watchtower listens ...
The Speakers watch
Fairies whisper
Demons quake,
Angels guard the Cannabis Souls ...
freely dance under the red sun's echoes ...
Limelight sprinkles
as your blooming fire warms
through your voices of songs.
As children scatter, kittens play,
thus the Spirit soars
And flying limbs with harmonies dance.

Merry girls dancing, flying stockings
Mermaids a' leaping, shooting champagne
Gentlemen swimming, hurling limbs
Kisses flowing, cupid swims
Clouds painting, pictures forming
Children jumping, reaching high
Creatures chasing, nature thriving
Sand dunes melting, lollies licking
Sun rays ticking, ticking by ...

And the Abyss opens
The Screaming, Drowning Child Whirls
Your Wasteland fears
Your Devastated years
Fly torpedoes
Fire arrows
The War Drums assemble
The Guns Power Lightning Spears
Skylines feel and gears whisk
The Rising Shining.

A Tribute to Sir Robert Peel 2ⁿᵈ Baronet FRS and Our Bobbies On The Beat

Piercing Blue Eyes Interject
And Soothingly Submerge
Betwixt In an Almighty Game of Spot The Difference
In the Ocean of Human Motions.

Piercing Blue Eyes delvingly intercept the depths of human time.
Askance at the Chances
Views of Time Tumble To and Fro
And Thy Trusty Troop Formations Gather
Sojourning Under Thy Guiding Gaze of Gallant Blue Eyes.

Corrosive and Corrupt Souls Lost - Direct!
Enamelled Fated Fingertips silently drumming
Their Fingerprints Quietly Bashing Away
Masterful Hands from Elegant Sprightly Limbs
Clutch and Withdraw Trouble Inked Claws of Lost Souls
Shields Art In Honour
Enact Clauses, Duty And Power.

Though Lost Souls Snigger and Jibe
Weathering In all the Skies of Seasons
Thy Incisive Wit and Intuitive Speed March The Lost Souls
Into Whimpering Slumbers of Defeat
As Submission Rules OK!

Blue Eyes Blooming Cupped In Knowledge
Quench Thirsts for Data In
The Unobtrusive Drinking of Secrets Locked

Beware Now - Nakedly Stare
Prised Open and Born
Secrets Shelled Are Captioned In Ink and Blunt Celluloid
Risen from the Grave Now Shelved.

Moonlight Sips Dawn and Dusk
Bequeathing Issues of Godspeed
Upon Thy Honourable Protecting Heart
Elegant Sprightly Limbs Adorn
Sunshine Blue Eyes
Masterly Glancing for SOS Echoes.

Thee and Thy Toiling Troops Slyly Sniff The Ride
The Chase To Rescue - Hounding
Bounding and Springing Across Lanes, Bridges and Gates
Arresting Disorders
Maintaining Borders
Thus Chillingly Conveying
Subtle Sentiments and Kindly Whispers
Soaked In Kismet Truths With Karmic Gifts.

God In A Box or Jack In The Box

Solid is the darkness
Upon your heartless souls
and whimpering limbs.
Liquid Terror
and
Gaseous Joy
bleed through the ghostly air
on concrete roads - Mystifying Rovers,
Whilst Ramblers streets
with topaz amber encrust
and gold swims the earth.

Spririt, Fright, Catch, Touch,
Ha ha ha
placidly ruling
thy iron organs of heart.

In buildings, wherein, entombed
elusive beneficaries of lying lords
weave majestically their
shallow deeds.

There, Candles Weep,
Heaven Weeps
and Anger Riseth
as Hypocrites Oath
silently
conquers the Church.

Wake OH Awake - Church
and let Justice Stamp
it's High Boot
upon your hardened
molten turned hearts.

THEN
Glory Splash Glory
or
Meet Thy Maker
with Death's sweet STING.

Sunshine Spiders

Blood stained scattered brewing rain
Pinches sunlight from it's maze
Forging alliances with Humans and Beasts
Of crawlies creepy Shunning the Earth
Instead Making Out In Our Beds
Crawling - Creepily Rising - Chasing Limbed Mammalian Prey
Crawlies creepily dine, slurping Human blood.

Sun Worshippers Kiss of Death
Is Kismet with Arachnid's Killing Sting
Whilst Glorious Snow Sadly Peters
Wind and Rain Exhilaratingly Scream
Power Upon Power

Burnt Scorched Sunlit Doom
Is a searing SOS Cry
Of Birds, Butterflies, Ladybirds and the Honourable Honey Bees
For Limbed Mammalians - Callously Coldly
In Selfish Horror
Perpetuate Plague and Pestilence
And Stealingly Swipe
The Reapers Scythe
To These Beloved Species

All Things Bright and Beautiful
Not Hymned No More - See
All Creatures Great and Small
All Things Wise and Wonderful Fall
Calling Perilously To Their Maker
For Sunlit Selfish Sun - Worshippers Songs
Spells Revelation.

Hospital Letter

I wrote this letter when I was fifteen years old and a patient in a Children's Ward of a hosptial.

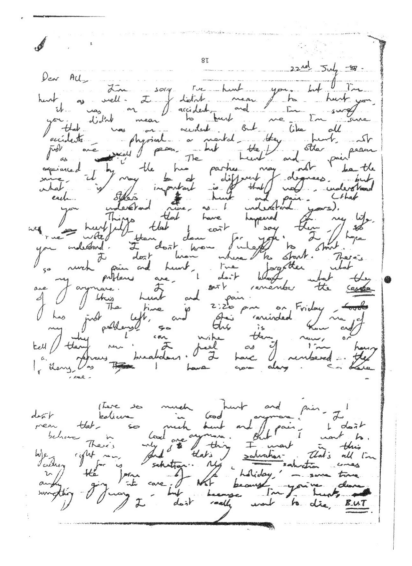

...if the only way to get rid of the hurt and the pain is by suicide (death) then I am willing, prepared and serious to do that. Believe me if these things don't get better, next time I'll make sure it works. I feel like taking a knife and cutting my chest open and taking all the hurt and pain out.

Have you ever felt like that. So bad. Cause this is how I feel, and I'm only 15. What a life. I have both parents and 3 brothers & 2 sisters, but I feel as if I've never had a family. You ask me, how can I come to you, when something's wrong, how can I, when you have hurt me.

1) Tell you what's wrong with our family. I feel as if there is no love. You've never hugged or kissed me. Never praised me, as far as I can remember. Or put it this way, you've never praised me, when I felt you should. I believe love is to love someone as the person they are. To love someone is to love their soul, their spirit. Which means their personality, who and what they really are. To love someone doesn't mean to love the person that you want them to be, because by doing that your making someone else a part of your self. Hence your not really loving that other person at all their spirit. Your also not allowing the other person's soul to be. It's just superficial. Your just denying them their life, in an only to turn hour yourself and make yourself secure and feel better. That is why they always say, you must love yourself because you can't give it.

This is how I feel. I feel as if you don't love me. I feel as if you don't really love me, that's a fact, but I don't really know which makes me think you don't love me. It's always what you want, how you want me to be, think, feel, love, what I want, or feel. That's wrong about love. Never...

that I've just write, I feel that is the situation between us. I want you to love me not the person you want me to be, because I am not that person, never will be, and don't want to be.

You're always shouting at me and criticising me. Never hugged or kissed me, as far as back I can remember, and that is since I was 5. Everybody ever arrives need to be hugged and loved. So what's wrong with doing that to me. You've hurt me so much by doing this, that I feel guilty being alive. I feel guilty breathing this air, this oxygen. I feel as if I don't deserve this life. You've put me down so much. Also, I'm scared of having a relationship with anyone, man or woman. I'm scared of meeting new people, because I'm scared of being hurt. Having relationships with someone means that sometime in that relationship you're going to be hurt. I think. I'm not quite sure. But that's how I feel.

I don't want your love, it all feels dirty and sick. Please don't love me, I mean. There is one more reason why I don't want you, and that's because . . . .

My culture CONTRADICTS my religion. Give you an example shall I? Sikhism (what you claim to be) believes some all I mean one of the things it holds for more than anything else, is that everyone is equal. Man — woman, — rich — poor. You are equal. The Indian culture believes that you are not equal. If you are a woman you are a slave to the rest of the world. If you are poor, you are a slave. It is sexist and racist. If there is one other place in the world apartheid is supported, it is in the indian community. You are not allowed to be yourself. you live by an image, or status, especially if you are a Asian. I can't live like that. I am a totally liberal person. You have to accept that. and allow me live a totally liberal wife. But I'm warning you. It wont be very good for the indian community. But if you love me. then you'll do that. Since to love someone properly is to love them, their soul, mind. not the person you want them to be, or you have made them. It's like living in a concentration camp - living in an indian community. Never allowed to be yourself. Always somebody else. well - atleast in my family anymore. I would agree with you if I oblige. if the person I wanted to be was going to hurt someone, or myself. But I ain't. I am anti-apartheid, anti-racist and anti-sexist, and liberal. And that's my life. Not the indian community or my family. Look how marriages are arranged. What are they in terms of money, social-class etc. Nothing but things. They say nothing about the person really. And then "you cry and marry, when your daughters marry. I don't feel sorry for you. You bring problems on yourself. Arranged marriages are not against the Sikh religion, got nothing to do with them. I know. I read it in a book which gave me. If your daughters married by their own will, you wouldn't have any problems or worries. because you'd know they were happy. You bring your problems on yourself - It's the somebody gives them to you. It's the way you live. If you chose to live by the Sikh religion properly, you wouldn't have half as many problems. Some of my Sikh friends at school are proper Sikhs, and live their life according to their religion, and live freely

(3).

to this culture

"I'm ... my ... friends of these sikh
jaunties are going to be cleverer and
bigger because they want to be ... and
have been encouraged. They are also
cuddled, kissed, and praised and rarely
shouted at or criticised. Why can't I
be like that. Since when have you
ever encouraged me to be someone,
have a career I mean or listen to
what I want.

Enough of this problem now. I could
go on for ages, with this one. But I
hope I've given a rough idea.
Let's summarize it shall we?

I don't love you because you've hurt
me, always shouting and criticising, no hugs,
or kisses. Since I've been so, as I
can remember. I mean I've grown up
feeling I don't love you. It's nothing new
I've never loved you. I know what
it is — but never felt it, or rarely have.
Your culture contradicts your religion.
And I can't live like that. I can't live
two lives. And before I can
belong to my religion I must find
a faith and believe in God. I haven't
got any faith. And so I can't believe in
God. All this hurt and pain.

Next problem.

2). P. T. O.

(You can't die for someone so why live their
life for them) D. H. .... Lawrence. (favourite writer)
True I agree, if I had cancer you
can't take it out of my body and put it
into yours. So don't live this life for me?
Remember
'Our's is essentially a tragic age. but we believe
emphatically not to be tragic about it.'
D. H. Lawrence.

43

2). I have been sexually abused. You won't believe me though. You don't have to help me, just believe me. If you wish to know any details then I will tell you. But I can't because it hurts.

One is a cousin. (male).
One is a woman who was friends. well supposed to be friends.

You know which is the hardest. the sex abuse. because this is what I've write least about. Because

IT's <u>SICH</u> AND I <u>HATE</u> IT.

and I can't write it. because it's <u>sick</u>, dirty and horrible.

I will tell you about #2 other things. and . I can't I haven't got the strength. It's hard to tell someone something — when it hurts. But it's <u>even harder</u> when you have to face the person whose hurt you. or someone near/ close to the person whose hurt you.

4.

P.S.

N.B.

My only regret is that I wish I had spoken earlier. Save myself so much hurt and pain — and you so much hurt and pain. And ~~this~~ ~~it~~ ultimately I wouldn't lose a family and you a daughter.

I'm afraid that's the truth, and I cant go on living a lie — I'm sorry but you've lost me. Nothing's going to change what's happened. So just go. I dont want you. I feel suffocated in your ~~presence~~ presence.

Again my only regret is that I wish I had spoken earlier. Save myself so much hurt and ~~pain~~ — and you. But this is it.

Hey listen:

"And God shall wipe all tears from their eyes, and there shall be no more death. neither sorrow nor crying. and neither shall there be any more pain.

For 'Neath the cold sand ~~we~~ dreamed of death, but woke at dawn to see in glory the

45

bright the morning star ".

Like he said.

' Ours is essentially a tragic age
but we decline emphatically not to
be tragic about it ".

Hospital Letter

I wrote this letter when I was fifteen years old and a patient in a Children's Ward of a hospital where the Consultant Paediatrician Dr Kalra and the Child Psychiatrist Dr Solomon saved my life and granted me sanctuary. I have not amended the spelling or grammar, it is as I wrote it aged fifteen and traumatised.

22nd July '88

Dear All,

I'm sorry I've hurt you but I'm hurt as well. I didn't mean to hurt you it was an accident and I'm sure you didn't mean to hurt me. I'm sure that was an accident. But like all accidents, physical or mental, they hurt, not just one person but the other person as well. The hurt and pain experienced by the two parties may not be the same, it may be at different degrees, but what is important is that we understand each other's hurt and pain. (That you understand mine, as I understand yours.)

Things that have happened in my life are so hurtful that I can't say them so I've wrote them down for you. I hope you understand. I don't know where to start.

I don't know where to start. There's so much pain and hurt, I've forgotten what my problems are, I don't know what they are anymore. I can't remember the cause of this hurt and pain.

The time is 2:20pm on Friday, C has just left, and she's reminded me of my problems so this is how and why I can write them now, or tell them now. I feel as if I'm having a nervous breakdown. I have remembered the problems as I have gone along. So here goes.

There's so much hurt and pain, I don't believe in God anymore. I mean that, so much hurt and pain, I don't believe in God anymore. But I want to.

There's only one thing I want in this life right now, and that's salvation.

47

That's all I'm asking for is salvation. My salvation comes in the form of a 'holiday' – some time away, going into care. Not because you've done something wrong, but because I'm hurt.

I don't really want to die, BUT if the only way to get rid of the hurt and pain is by suicide (death) then I am willing, prepared and serious to do that.

Believe me if things don't get better; next time I'll make sure it works. I feel like taking a knife, and cutting my chest open, and taking all the hurt and pain out.

Have you ever felt like that, so bad? 'Cause this is how I feel, and I'm only 15. What a life. I have both parents and 3 brothers, & 2 sisters, but I feel as if I've never had a family. You ask me, to come to you when something's wrong, how can I, when you have hurt me.

1. Tell you what's wrong with our family. I feel as if there is no love. You've never hugged or kissed me. Never praised me, as far as I can remember. Or put it this way, you've never praised me, when I felt you should. I believe love is to love someone, as the person they are.

To love someone is to love their soul, their spirit. Which means their personality, who and what they really are. To love someone doesn't mean to love the person that you want them to be, because by doing that you're making someone else a part of you or someone you want them to be. Hence you're not really loving that other person at all. You're also not allowing the other person's soul, spirit, live it's full potential, you're in fact denying them their life and in turn loving yourself and making yourself securer and feel better.

That is why they always say you must love yourself before you can give it.

This is how I feel. I feel as if you don't love me. I know you love me, that's a fact, but I don't feel it which makes me think you don't love me. It's always what you want, how you want me to be, think, feel, look. Never what I want or feel. That writing about love that I've just wrote, I feel that is the situation between us. I want you to love me not the person you want me to be, because I am not that person, never will be, and don't want to be.

You're always shouting at me and criticising me. Never hugged or kissed me, as far as back I can remember, and that is since I was 5. Everybody even animals need to be hugged and loved. So what's wrong with doing that to me. You've hurt me so much by doing this that I feel guilty being alive. I feel guilty breathing this air, this oxygen. I feel as if I don't deserve this life. You've put me down so much. Also, I'm scared of having a relationship with anyone, man or woman. I'm scared of meeting new people because I'm scared of being hurt. Having relationship with someone means that sometime in that relationship you're going to be hurt. I think. I'm not quite sure. But that's how I feel.

I don't want your love, it feels dirty and sick. Please don't love me, it hurts.

There is one more reason why I don't want you and that's because.......
My culture CONTRADICTS my religion. Give you an example shall I?

Sikhism (what you claim to be) believes above all, I mean one of the things it stands for, more than anything else, is that everyone is equal. Man, woman, rich, poor. You are equal. The Indian culture believes that you are not equal. If you are a woman you are a slave to the rest of the world. If you are poor you are a slave. It is sexist and racist. If there is one other place in the world apartheid is supported it is in the Indian community. You are not allowed to be yourself, you live by an image or status, especially if you are a woman. I can't live like that. I am a totally liberal person. You have to accept that and allow me live a totally liberal life. But I'm warning you it won't look very good in the Indian community. But if you love me then you'll do that. Since to love someone properly is to love them, their soul, mind not the person you want them to be or you have made them. It's like living in a concentration camp, living in an Indian community. Never allowed to be yourself. Always somebody else. Well, at least in my family anyway. I would agree with you and oblige. If the person I wanted to be was going to hurt someone, or myself. But it isn't. I am anti-apartheid, anti-racist and anti-sexist, and liberal. And that's my life. Not the Indian community or my family. Look how marriages are arranged. In terms of money, social class, etc. What are they nothing but things. They say nothing about the person really. And then you cry and worry when your daughters marry. I don't feel sorry for you. You bring your problems on yourself.

Arranged marriages are not against the Sikh religion, got nothing to do with them, I know, I read in a book which J gave me. If your daughters married by they're own will, you wouldn't have any problems or worries because you'd know they were happy. You bring your problems on yourself, nobody gives them to you. It's the way you live. If you choose to live by the Sikh religion properly, you wouldn't have half as many problems. Some of my friends at school are proper Sikhs, and live their life according to their religion, and live rarely to their culture. Some of my friends of these Sikh families are going to be doctors and lawyers because they want to be and have been encouraged. They are also cuddled, kissed and praised and rarely shouted at or criticised. Why can't we be like that? Since when have you ever encouraged me to be someone, have a career, I mean, or listen to what I want.

Enough of this problem now. I could go on for ages, with this one. But I hope I've given a rough idea.

Let's summarise it shall we?

I don't love you because you've hurt me, always shouting and criticising, no hugs or kisses. Since I've been 5, as I can remember. I mean I've grown up feeling I don't love you. It's nothing new I've never loved you. I know what it is- but never felt it, or rarely have.

Your culture contradicts your religion. And I can't live like that. I can't live two lives. And before I can belong to any religion I must find faith and believe in God. I haven't got any faith and so I can't believe in God. All this hurt and pain.

Next problem.

You can't die for someone so why live their life for them D. H. Lawrence. (favourite writer).

True I agree if I had cancer you can't take it out of my body and put it into yours. So don't live this life for me.

Remember 'Ours is essentially a tragic age, but we believe emphatically not to be tragic about it.' D. H. Lawrence.

I have been sexually abused. You won't believe me though. You don't have to help me, just believe me. If you wish to know any details then G will tell you. But I can't because it hurts.

One is a cousin (male).

One is a woman who was friends, well supposed to be friends.

You know which is the hardest the sex abuse, because this is what I've wrote least about. Because

IT'S SICK AND I HATE IT.

and I can't write it because it's sick & dirty and horrible.

G will tell you about & 2 other things and I can't I haven't got the strength. It's hard to tell someone something when it hurts. But it's even harder when you have to face the person who's hurt you, or someone near/ close to the person who's hurt you.

P.S.

N.B.

My only regret is that I wish I had spoken earlier. Save myself so much hurt and pain - and you so much hurt and pain. And ultimately I wouldn't lose a family and you a daughter.

I'm afraid that's the truth, and I can't go on living a lie. I'm sorry but you've lost me. Nothing's going to change what's happened. So just go.

I don't want you. I feel suffocated in your presence.

Again my only regret is that I wish I had spoken earlier. Save myself so much hurt and pain, and you. But this is it.

Hey listen:

"And God shall wipe all tears from their eyes, and there shall be no more death, neither sorrow nor crying and neither shall there be any more pain.

For 'Neath the cold sand we dreamed of death, but woke at dawn to see in glory the bright the morning star."

Like he said.

"Ours is essentially a tragic age but we believe emphatically not to be tragic about it."

Epilogue

I owe my life to my teachers, doctors, music, James, Liberty and Arthur, the authors Agatha Christie, P G Wodehouse, Graham Greene and D H Lawrence and my faith in God, without whom I would not have survived and together with my faith in Christ and my spirituality, these gifts from Christ helped me keep my sanity.

When I wrote the poem 'Haunted Saturdays' I cried so much I could not see the paper I was writing on. It all poured out. This poem and some of the others do not contain any grammar. That is on purpose. The lack of grammar is part of the poem, in that it is there to convey when the sexual abuse took place. It is the four-year-old child in me trying to explain and understand – and four-year-old children do not use grammar. Four-year-old children do not use question marks.

The poem 'Consent' was inspired by a dream; I dreamt of the woman who sexually abused me and in this dream I was very angry with her and I shouted at her, hence the angry words I wrote down in the poem on the day I had the dream.

I remember acutely days when I was six years old and I was standing beside my teacher Mrs Vernon and I desperately wanted to tell her about the sexual abuse but I could not and the reason why I could not is because I lacked the vocabulary to describe or explain sexual abuse to anyone. I knew what my nose, mouth, eyes, ears, hands, arms, legs, feet and toes were but nobody had ever told me what my vagina is called. If I had known that my vagina is called a 'vagina', then I think on those desperate days I would have told my teacher Mrs Vernon. That's why I think all children should learn the proper names for their vagina and penis because that in itself will help protect the child from abuse. Nevertheless, I am extremely grateful to Mrs Vernon, the Headmistress Mrs Ady and all the staff at Neachells Lane Infant school because their love and devotion helped me cope with being abused. They also taught me the Lord's Prayer and hymns. Learning about Jesus Christ and this spirituality helped me beyond explanation – it helped me to cope with being abused and gave me hope. The devotion and guidance of my infant school teachers was exemplary and saved my life.

Mine is a story of being sexually abused from the age of four by a woman and later on at the age of nine by an Indian male known to the family. It began really because my family never loved me. They being a strict Indian family, were disappointed I was a girl and not a boy. Furthermore, when my mother was pregnant with me she became diabetic. I was blamed for this misfortune and was repeatedly told it was my fault. Thus I had to be punished and was never loved by any member of my family except for my late father. The astonishing truth is that men and women sexually abuse children; furthermore, it is my observation from my research that paedophiles prey upon and target children who are unloved and forsaken by their families. I am not referring here to stranger danger abductions but rather sexual abuse where the abuser is known to the child and family.

I once had a conversation with a doctor regarding my ill-health as a child. I was a very sickly child and unfortunately missed a lot of school too. This was very distressing for me as I absolutely loved school – school was my haven and sanctuary. My doctor and I discussed how the childhood sexual abuse I suffered resulted in my being a sickly child because every time I was being sexually abused my abuser was infecting my body with her germs, viruses and bacteria, even resulting in hospitalisation once due to a fever and of course I was merely a child and my body was unable to cope.

I cannot remember the very first time I was sexually abused, not even in dreams. When I was sixteen, twenty and thirty this was frustrating and distressing for me however every doctor I spoke to explained to me that I cannot remember the beginning of the childhood sexual abuse because my brain has blanked the initial trauma in order to protect my mind. I accept this now and marvel at the wonders of the brain; I know that others whom have been abused or suffered great trauma are also paradoxically protected by psychogenic amnesia

I was born into a very strict Indian family that believed girls should be married off at sixteen and should not be allowed to study, to read books and to go to university. However, it was this dream of going to university and reading books that helped me keep my sanity when I was the one born 'in the asylum' as it were! As we venture forth into the twenty-first century I hope the Indian community and culture evolves and learns to cherish and love their daughters, respecting their marital and educational rights. Indeed, even boys and homosexuals are victims of forced marriages. It took me over twenty years to learn and discover there are Indian families who do love their daughters and who are not disappointed they have a girl and not a boy. This was a revelation to me! Still, to this very day, female infanticide and forced abortions – due to the baby being a girl and not a boy – are devastating crimes in India and across the world within the diaspora from the Indian subcontinent. I know, as a member of the Indian race, that treating females as subhumans and second-class citizens leads to female abortions and forced marriages which are problems amongst all these communities: Hindus, Sikhs and Muslims; very often those outside the Indian race are unaware and indeed shocked when I try to explain this to them. However thankfully the British Government Home Office Forced Marriage Unit recognises that forced marriages are a problem amongst all these cultures and that the problem is purely cultural and not religious whatsoever. Culture is a living, thriving, evolving phenomenon. Within the last hundred years it was illegal to practise homosexuality or to commit suicide – and indeed for women to vote in Great Britain; thus, the degrading hatred that Indian women and girls suffer worldwide is one that can and should evolve into love, freedom, dignity and respect, with marital and educational rights for Indian females, whatever the country of our birth.

When in the Indian community worldwide are baby girls no longer going to be aborted because of their gender? When are Indian girls and women no longer going to commit suicide or be murdered because their dowries are deemed insufficient and pitiful? When are Indian girls going to be celebrated from birth instead of being hated for not being a boy? When is the Indian community and culture worldwide going to learn to cease their misogyny? I also give my support to homosexuals within the Indian community worldwide, all too often they too are forced into marriages or driven to suicide or even murdered.

Outside of the Indian community worldwide people will find this unbelievable: within Indian culture there is an inverted racism also known as colourism. In the business of arranged marriages, some Indian people – not all, only some – prefer women with paler skin. In fact, the whiter the skin, the less brown the skin is, the more marriageable and prestigious she is deemed to these people. Throughout my childhood my family constantly chided me for (amongst other complaints) having a darker brown skin than the rest of them and they were forever telling me that because my skin is a darker brown they will have great difficulty in marrying me off! In 1994 or 1995 BBC Radio 4 broadcast a documentary exploring the world of arranged marriages in India and the people they spoke to in this documentary openly admitted that for some Indian people a bride with very light brown skin or white skin is highly prized and sought after! At that point, listening to the radio, I felt vindication and relief that I am not the only Indian girl who has suffered racism from her own people and family because her skin is darker than theirs. When I went to India aged nine years old, all my family could worry and complain about was how dark my skin would become because of the tan I would pick up and how long it would take for the tan to disappear! I know it beggars belief to the rest of us! I observe that, as a rule, Indian men do not suffer such demoralising and degrading sexist nor racist objectification from their own ethnic race and are neither treated as chattel.

I ask two things of the Indian community worldwide – please do not turn your backs on your daughters, sons, brothers and sisters who have been raped or sexually abused and please do not force them into marriages. I was a Sikh girl who was sexually abused from the age of four and I am innocent and I have nothing to be ashamed of.

One of my favourite authors, P G Wodehouse, dealt with the subject of forced marriages in his novel Bill the Conqueror, published in 1924. Wodehouse perfectly describes the terror and petrified state of the heroine as she tries to escape a forced marriage. I found it a harrowing read as I knew that P G Wodehouse was spot on!

For me it all began before I was born in 1930s India. Apparently, it is an infamous story in my late father's home-town; everyone knows what happened to him when he was five years old. My father's parents were landowners and had an estate. When my father was five years old his parents – my paternal grandparents were killed. My father's paternal uncle (my great-uncle) stole my father's estate and inheritance, using him as a servant and slave on his own estate and in his own home. He never sent him to school and used to beat him. The other servants on the estate looked after my father and he taught himself to read and write. When he was old enough, he joined the RAF. After he had finished his service, the evil uncle came back and asked my father for a lot of money, pretending to be poor. My late father took pity on his evil uncle, fell for the sob-story and forgave him, giving him his hard-earned self-made fortune. The uncle disappeared with my father's money and never returned. When my father realised he had been betrayed and swindled again by the same uncle, he had a nervous breakdown and never recovered. He was unable to protect me and look after me due to his mental illness but he did state unequivocally that I should be able to marry when I wished and to whoever I chose and that I should be allowed to attend university. For this statement that my father made to the family I am eternally grateful.

The thing is, my family not loving me and abusing me opened the door to paedophiles sexually abusing me, as they will prey upon children who are unloved and forsaken. Thus, the evil my great-uncle committed in stealing my father's estate and inheritance culminated in my own sexual abuse forty years later. My father loved me but he was mentally too ill to help me and look after me. When I told my family that I had been sexually abused they tried to force me to marry a man from India so that he could come and live in Great Britain and to prevent me from going to university. However, even though in India the female age of consent for marriage is eighteen years of age, in Great Britain, I a British Indian schoolgirl had to fight against being forced to leave school and forced into a marriage under the age of eighteen to a man from India!

I was born a Sikh and was baptised a Catholic on the 25th March 1989 at Our Lady of Perpetual Succour Church in Moss Side, Manchester, aged sixteen. British Law declares that all subjects have a legal right to change their religion or join a religion (if one is born into an atheist family) from the age of sixteen. I have believed in Jesus Christ since I was five years old when I learnt about Christ at school. I believe there is one God and that people of all religions – Hindus, Jews, Sikhs, Buddhists, Christians, Muslims, Pagans and Atheists – are in Heaven. I also believe Hell and Purgatory exist, furthermore I believe in reincarnation, life has taught me that sometimes God sends a soul back. I have found it fascinating that throughout my life God has sent Hindus, Jews and Muslims to help me. A Hindu consultant paediatrician, Dr Deepak Kalra, saved me and gave me sanctuary. The child psychiatrist Dr Solomon understood me emphatically, perfectly and compassionately. A Muslim consultant psychiatrist Dr W Ahmed understood me, helped me to disclose aspects of the abuse I could not comprehend and utter previously and he helped me to find peace. The best landlord I ever had was a Muslim, Mr S Saieed, he gave me a home when I needed somewhere to live without asking for rent or a deposit in advance. He waited patiently for me to have the money to pay him and he never asked me any intrusive questions. He was a perfect knight and gentleman.

My faith in Jesus Christ has enabled me to forgive my family and the people who sexually abused me, although I never want to see them again, they have taken too much already and it would distress me beyond belief. I appreciate and understand that something truly catastrophic must have occurred in the life of the woman who sexually abused me, I pity her and I forgive her completely. I wish her NO HARM whatsoever and I know that be it in this life or the next, God will save her mind, soul and spirit and she too will be released from her torment. Love and forgiveness are the bedrock of our civilisation.

'If you seek revenge dig two graves.' Chinese Proverb.

For me one of the greatest elements of Christianity is the concept of free will: the freedom to follow one's destiny and to be the person God created us to be, individually, personally and uniquely. I cherish that free will – the gift that allows each and every one of us to follow our unique destiny. Of course, free will and freedom must always be twinned with responsibility at every level, otherwise anarchy will prevail. Through Christ I have discovered and gained my humanity, destiny, femininity as well as my educational and marital rights and self-autonomy as a female of the species. Whilst I did not enjoy these gifts as a Sikh, I know there are Sikh, Hindu and Muslim families who do cherish, love, trust and respect their daughters and whom are afforded their liberty.

Life is very strange indeed. When I was fifteen years old I was the patient of a consultant paediatrician and child psychiatrist and yet fifteen years later, in my capacity as a SEND careers adviser I was seated alongside headteachers, paediatricians and child psychiatrists in case conferences. Lo and behold, these highly-esteemed professionals looked to me and sought my professional advice and solutions to help our patients and students. I never divulged to my colleagues secrets about my childhood as I recognised it would prove unprofessional and even in child protection and forced marriage training at work I kept silent and still. I will never forget the warm welcome I received from the teachers, students and their families in the schools and colleges I worked in. I was only able to carry out my professional duties because of God's salvation, my education, the NHS and the top-notch training I received from colleagues in my probationary year; this achievement is a monument to all of them.

All of us are dealt a set of cards at our birth and it is up to us as to how we play them. There is always someone worse off than ourselves and there are both adults and children who have suffered far worse sexual abuse than I did. This frightens me and my heart goes out to them.

I have found great peace and understanding through astrology; I had my birth charts drawn up by Tony Hyland and Robert Currey, who I think are the best astrologers in England. Their accuracy is breathtaking and it has moved me to tears. They both patiently listened to me on the telephone as we worked together to understand the planetary implications in my birth chart. It was they who discovered and exposed the terrible, dark secrets in my birth chart: firstly, that I would suffer a catastrophic loss of family in my teenage years. I left my family at sixteen and have been financially independent since. Secondly, due to the position of two planets at the time of my birth, I was in grave danger of being sexually abused. The astrologers explained to me that I was in grave danger of sexual violence but since it had already happened the danger had been exhausted. It need not have happened, it could have been prevented: what was needed was extra protection and care (and I think some martial arts training to establish confidence with oneself physically and psychologically) and for my family to love me and never leave me alone with anyone. Such is the astonishing value of astrology. It is an invaluable and priceless gift from God.

Likewise, the chirologist Johnny Fincham is astonishingly and breathtakingly accurate too and my sessions with him have been invaluable, helping me to understand and learn and in doing so moved me to tears. When I was about fourteen years old, an Indian woman came to the house and quite happily read everyone's palms but when she came to me, she held my hands and studied my palms for a couple of minutes and then quite forcefully dropped them and exclaimed, "I cannot tell you, I cannot tell you!" but Johnny Fincham and I know!

My favourite musicians, whose music has been healing and therapeutic for me, are as follows:

- Judas Priest
- Black Sabbath
- Hawkwind

- Motörhead
- Electric Light Orchestra
- 10cc
- Supertramp
- Paul Simon and Art Garfunkel
- Barclay James Harvest
- Bob Marley
- David Bowie
- Led Zeppelin
- Pink Floyd
- Tinie Tempah's song 'Written in the Stars'
- Ludovico Einaudi
- Thomas Tallis
- Hildegard of Bingen

Music and the Alchemy of Friendship with a splash of Noah's wine is the elixir of life.

Larissa and Liberty by the late Audrey Schwartz 1974-1997.

Throughout my poems and in my hospital letter I have written about being suicidal. For me the number one issue arising from childhood sexual abuse is the fact it leaves one feeling suicidal. The first time in my life I wanted to commit suicide I was about ten years old, I grew up feeling suicidal and I started phoning The Samaritans from the age of twelve. The cruel irony and tragedy is that my oldest and closest friend Audrey committed suicide for reasons that are inexplicable to all those who were blessed to know her. I will never forgive myself for her suicide. I was supposed to help her by talking to her about feeling suicidal because I had been abused but I procrastinated and failed to tell her the truth. I was embarrassed and ashamed as a teenager and as a young adult I wanted to pretend all was hunky dory because her life seemed perfect and I wanted to concentrate on the future and not look at the past which I was escaping. Even though Audrey had not been abused and hence our reasons for being suicidal differed, the mere fact we were both suicidal might have helped her to know that she can seek help and she is not alone, that I too understand what it is like to be suicidal. I was supposed to open up to her and hold her hand in this regard so that she would have known she is not alone - we are not alone. Twenty years later the pain of her suicide is as devastating as it was the day it happened and I failed as a friend to reach out to her. Since her tragic death she has come to me in dreams, I know she is at peace and in Heaven, giving her loving support. Please do not make my mistake - talk when you feel suicidal, you never know it might save someone else too.

Acknowledgements

With every Quark, Strangeness and Charm of my being I thank you with heart-felt gratitude....

Nicola Mackin FRAS and aSys Publishing www.asys-publishing.co.uk

Piers Corbyn MSc (astrophysics), ARCS FRAS, FRMet - Wow! Such enlightenment is found at www.weatheraction.com

www.truetorahjews.org - Thank you for educating me; you are all great Jewish Theologians. The Holy Spirit - God's Spirit speaks through you and you are indeed vessels of the Lord God Almighty. My dear, sweet Holy Rabbis it's Psalm 27 and Psalm 37. Godspeed to you all.

Dr John Coutts www.johncoutts.eu

Martyn Green

Mick and Val Windsor

Marie and Stephen Collier

Aurelie Barthel

Sophie Nicolas

Greta Lencickaite

Pamela Davies

Liberty G V Saxby-Bridger, Arthur G K Saxby-Bridger and James Saxby-Bridger

Christine Hewitt

Elaine and Tony Ring

Michael Wall. It is in your home and in your presence I wrote the poem, 'As Big As The Bad Has Been, As Big The Good Will Be'. I didn't even have any paper with me upon which to scribble down this poem but you saved the day and speedily supplied the writing paper.

John Hamer

Prof John Bastin MA PhD FRAS

Phil Lockwood www.phil-lockwood.com

Liz Balkwill PS AFAS IEA www.lizbalkwill.com

Preeti Shenoy www.preetishenoy.com

Robert Currey www.equinoxastrology.com

Johnny Fincham www.johnnyfincham.com

Tony Hyland, Astrologer www.tonyhyland.com

India and her people; when I was nine years old I visited India and this was the first time in my life I experienced and witnessed devotion, kindness and acceptance from Indians. I will never forget your devotion, kindness and acceptance, it truly was an astonishing revelation for me. With love and God's blessings to India and her people.

My gratitude, love and patriotism "I vow to thee, my country" Great Britain

National Geographic and Ancestry DNA: It was a watershed moment in my life discovering my ancestry DNA: I am of Persian, North East Indian, Mediterranean, Russian, Finnish and Chinese descent. Extraordinarily when I was twelve years old I wrote to the Russian Embassy in London asking for a Russian pen friend and I got a book from the library to try and teach myself Russian, furthermore I love snow (and rain) it is my favourite weather. Looking back, in some way this was my Russian ancestors in my DNA - in my blood, popping up to say "Hello". We really are all the peoples of the Earth and the children of God. With love to my ancestry DNA cousins, I am amazed and deeply honoured to have you in my life: Namita Singh, Haseena Ali, Adila Ahmed and Bis Channey.

The late Michael Jamieson Bristow www.national-anthems.org

The National Association for People Abused In Childhood / NAPAC https://napac.org.uk

The Samaritans www.samaritans.org

www.gov.uk/guidance/forced-marriage

Lightning Source UK Ltd.
Milton Keynes UK
UKHW02f0637110218
317695UK00009B/125/P

9 781910 757956